1000 Shutters and Awnings

Jo Cryder

Schiffer Publishing Ltd
4880 Lower Valley Road Atglen, Pennsylvania 19310

Other Schiffer Books by Jo Cryder
1000 Fences and Gates
1000 Dormers

Other Schiffer Books on Related Subjects
Doors of Oaxaca. Devon Fekete
Traditional Mexican Style Exteriors. Donna McMenamin
Old World Inspiration for American Architecture. Richard S. Requa
Architectural Details from Victorian Homes. Stanley Schuler

Library of Congress Control Number: 2007928994

Type set in Aurora BdCn BT/Humanist 521 BT

ISBN: 978-0-7643-2711-7
Printed in China

Published by Schiffer Publishing Ltd.
4880 Lower Valley Road
Atglen, PA 19310
Phone: (610) 593-1777; Fax: (610) 593-2002
E-mail: Info@schifferbooks.com

In Europe, Schiffer books are distributed by
Bushwood Books
6 Marksbury Ave.
Kew Gardens
Surrey TW9 4JF England
Phone: 44 (0) 20 8392-8585; Fax: 44 (0) 20 8392-9876
E-mail: info@bushwoodbooks.co.uk
Website: www.bushwoodbooks.co.uk
Free postage in the U.K., Europe; air mail at cost.

Contents

Exterior Shutters

We have all seen exterior shutters on many buildings and houses. They look really nice, but have you ever wondered how many different kinds of shutters there are available? The one time I decided to put shutters on a home I went to a store and selected a set of ready-made unfinished colonial shutters from the variety they had to offer. I took them home, painted them and nailed them up on either side of the windows. When I was finished I thought they looked great. I learned a lot putting this book together that I would like to have known before selecting and installing those shutters. The photographs are accurate, but all the comments made are my own opinions.

Basically, exterior shutters fall into two categories: traditional colonial exterior shutters and hurricane or storm shutters. A popular use for colonial shutters is for decoration. Shutters are colorful. Shutters add dimension. Shutters enhance a window shape and size. When installing decorative colonial shutters, they are simply fixed in position (using nails or screws) on either side of a window, door or vent. There is no concern that they are installed on any type of structurally adequate framing members or using secure anchoring methods. Aside from aesthetics, there is a functional reason for shutters, to protect windows or doors from high winds and flying debris. These are working shutters.

To demonstrate the overall effect that exterior shutters can make on a structure, here are a few houses with exterior shutters in a variety of styles, colors, and designs. The houses shown here each have different shutter designs.

House with Shutters
The house shown here has two kinds of hurricane shutters in matching colors.

House with Shutters
This house has hurricane and colonial shutters in matching colors, adding more color to the residence. The hurricane shutters on the top row are called Bahama or Bermuda. The colonial shutters on the bottom are board and batten with diagonal batten. There is a pair of matching shutters available to protect the door.
Key West, Florida

House with Shutters
The shutters on the top two windows appear to be inset shutters.
Key West, Florida

House with Shutters
Key West, Florida

House with Shutters
You can tell the shape of the windows by the shape of the colonial louver shutters. There are radius louver shutters on the arched window.
Galveston Island, Texas

House with Shutters
Shutters protect and decorate the windows in this stately old Galveston mansion.
Galveston, Texas

House with Shutters
Notice the differences in window and cornice treatments on these two corresponding homes that are physically located next to each other.
Key West, Florida

House with Shutters
Key West, Florida

With the proper hardware and installation instructions, exterior colonial shutters can be mounted so they can be operable shutters. This will turn those "decorative shutters" into something that, when closed, will provide privacy, security, shade from the sun while allowing for air circulation, and protection against high winds, flying debris, and rain … and they will continue to be decorative as well. The following pictures will show you a sampling of some of the hardware that is available to turn decorative shutters into working shutters.

Exterior Colonial Shutter Hardware
A curl shutter tie back that is mounted at the bottom of the shutter holds the shutter in the open position.
Mackinac Island, Michigan

Exterior Colonial Shutter Hardware
One can appreciate the planning and ingenuity that went into the security of the shutters. There is one system to hold them open and another to secure them when they are closed. This system works with the use of a stick or bar placed in the brackets.
Florida Keys

Exterior Colonial Shutter Hardware
Heavy duty L-hinges are securing these shutters.
Key West, Florida

Exterior Colonial Shutter Hardware
This shutter has a typical shutter hinge system called a plate mount pintel.
Key West, Florida

Exterior Colonial Shutter Hardware
A shutter dog/holdback mounted near the top of the shutter holds the shutter in the open position. One advantage of placing the shutter dog/holdback higher up makes it out of reach for easy tampering.
Key West, Florida

Exterior Colonial Shutter Hardware
A shutter dog/holdback mounted at the bottom of the shutter holds the shutter in the open position.
Savannah, Georgia

Exterior Colonial Shutter Hardware
A close-up of a Belmont shutter dog/holdback mounted at the bottom of the shutter.
Savannah, Georgia

Exterior Colonial Shutter Hardware
An S-curve shutter dog/holdback is within easy reach to operate. This model has a spring to secure it in position.
Savannah, Georgia

Exterior Colonial Shutter Hardware
An S-curve shutter dog/holdback is within easy reach to operate.
Savannah, Georgia

Exterior Colonial Shutter Hardware
Savannah, Georgia

Exterior Colonial Shutter Hardware
These shutters have bolts that are used to secure the shutters when they are closed. These two sets of shutters are in the open position, so we can see the bolts from the outside.
Savannah, Georgia

Exterior Colonial Shutter Hardware
This appears to be the original shutter locking system on this home built in 1841.
Turkey Run State Park, Indiana

Exterior Colonial Shutter Hardware
These appear to be the original mortise mounting hinges on this home built in 1841.
Turkey Run State Park, Indiana

Exterior Colonial Shutter Hardware
Here's a delicate looking holdback effectively doing its job.
Bloomington, Illinois

The selection of hardware used to install operable colonial shutters will depend on whether the structure is an area prone to high winds and windborne debris, including hurricane prone regions, or is situated in milder climates. The choice must be made between decorative hardware and hardware that will provide a secure anchoring method.

In order to recognize if shutters are operable, look closely at the hardware, the size of the shutters versus the size of the window or door, and whether there are permanent obstacles to closing the shutters.

To become familiar with more of what is available, search for "exterior shutter hardware" on the internet. Be sure to follow manufacturer's instructions and guidelines when installing any type of shutter.

Exterior colonial and hurricane shutters are made out of a variety of materials, including vinyl, wood, wood composition, aluminum, fiberglass, and sheet metal. When purchasing shutters, specify to the craftsman or vendor whether they are going to be used as decorative shutters or as operable shutters. Some materials cannot be installed to function as operable shutters.

Although they are most popular on houses, cottages and vacation homes, shutters can be used on most any type of building, i.e., hotels, motels, banks, office buildings, apartments, condominiums and restaurants. The list goes on. Shutters can be made to cover different shapes of openings. They are used on windows, doors, vents, porches, and walkways. There will be many pictures showing their use on windows, vents, and doors, but the following pictures demonstrate the unique and delightful use of shutters on porches and walkways.

Exterior Colonial Shutters on Porches and Walkways
This is a view of the shutters from the inside. The shutters provide privacy on the exterior walkway where it intersects with another walkway that leads to a private area.
Key West, Florida

Exterior Colonial Shutters on Porches and Walkways
This is an outside view of shutters that are on a walkway at an intersection. The picture shows the privacy the shutters provide.
Key West, Florida

Exterior Colonial Shutters on Porches and Walkways
Louvered shutters provide privacy and shade on a porch.
Key West, Florida

Exterior Colonial Shutters on Porches and Walkways
Louver shutters are installed to provide the option of privacy and shade and can be opened easily.
Key West, Florida

Far left:
Exterior Colonial Shutters on Porches and Walkways
Louver shutters enclose a patio and walkway between a house and garage and provide privacy from a busy street.
Florida Keys

Left:
Exterior Colonial Shutters on Porches and Walkways
This louver shutter slides open for easy access from the front sidewalk.
Florida Keys

Exterior Colonial Shutters on Porches and Walkways
The louver shutters add privacy and shade at the corner of the porch where there is a cozy seating area.
Key West, Florida

Shutter Alternatives from FEMA

FEMA (Federal Emergency Management Agency) publishes a series, "Home Building Guide to Coastal Construction," that includes "Shutter Alternatives" technical fact sheet No. 26, FEMA 499/August 2005. This fact sheet provides general information about the installation and use of storm shutters in coastal areas. A free copy of the current edition of "Home Building Guide to Coastal Construction" can be obtained by calling the FEMA distribution center at 800-480-2520. It is also available on the FEMA website www.fema.gov.

Exterior Shutters Internet References

The craftsmen that are selling exterior shutters on the internet offer a great deal of information. Their websites explain the details for materials, designs, colors, styles, installation, hardware, and accessories. You can find them by going to your favorite search engine, and search for "exterior shutters", "hurricane shutters", and "storm shutters."

If you are interested in shutters to protect your home during storms, it's imperative that you go to the following internet site and the sites referenced at the end of the FEMA article you will find there: http://www.snopes.com/science/hurricane.asp

Sketches of Colonial and Hurricane Shutters

Below are sketches of the various designs of exterior shutters. Each sketch is identified with the section number where the pictures of that type of shutter can be found here in the book.

Sketches of Exterior Shutters
Colonial

Section 1. Creative Designs
Exterior shutters with individual and unique designs that have been independently crafted and/or personalized..

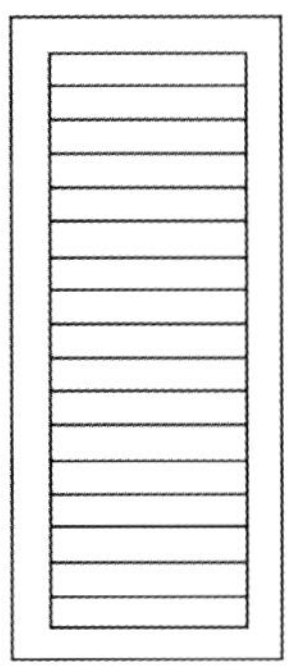

Section 2.
Single Frame with Fixed Louvers

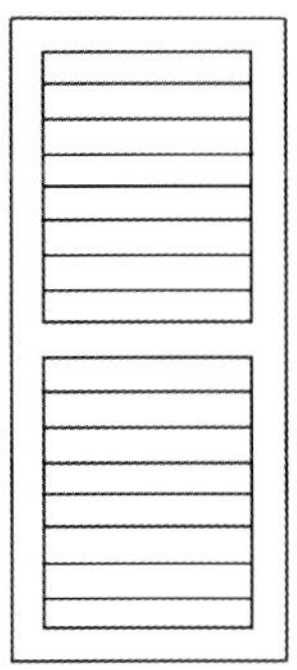

Section 3.
Divided Frame with Fixed Louvers

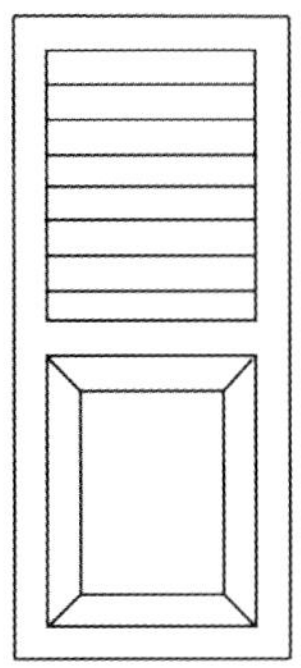

Section 4.
Combination Louver and Raised or Flat Panel

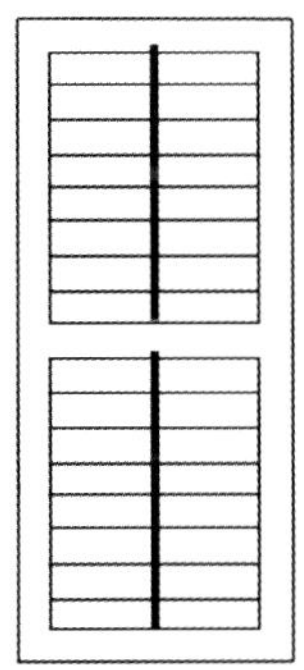

Section 5.
Adjustable Louvers with Tilt Rod

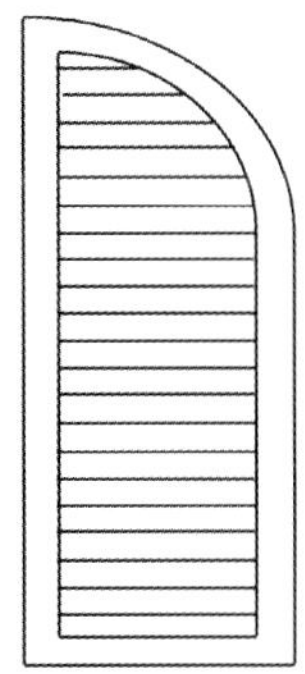

Section 6.
Shutters with Radius Top

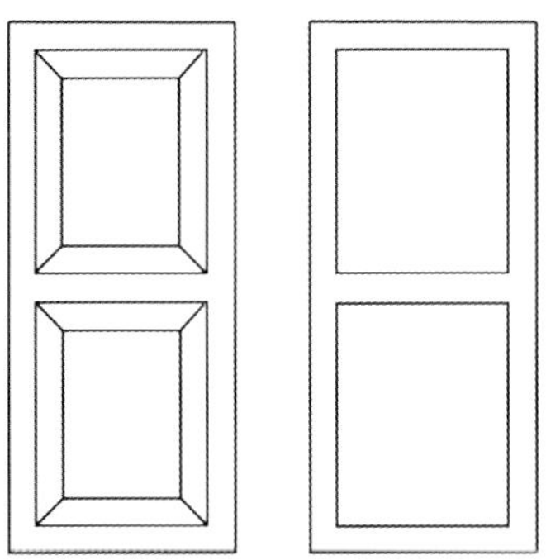

7. Colonial, Raised or Flat Panel

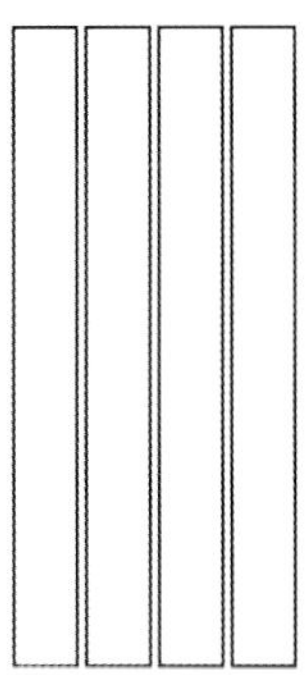

Section 8.
Board

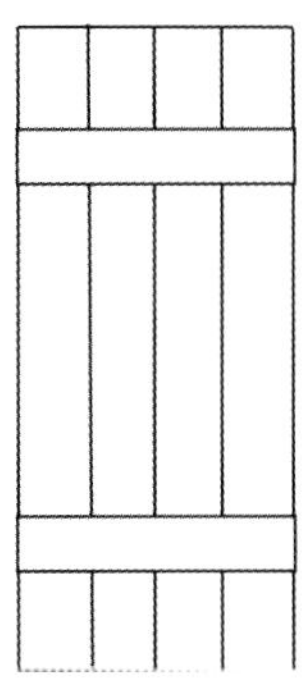

Section 9.
Board and Batton

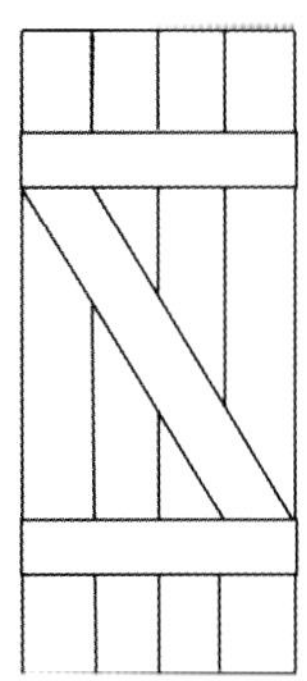

Section 10.
Board and Batton with Diagonal Batton

Sketches of Exterior Shutters
Hurricane

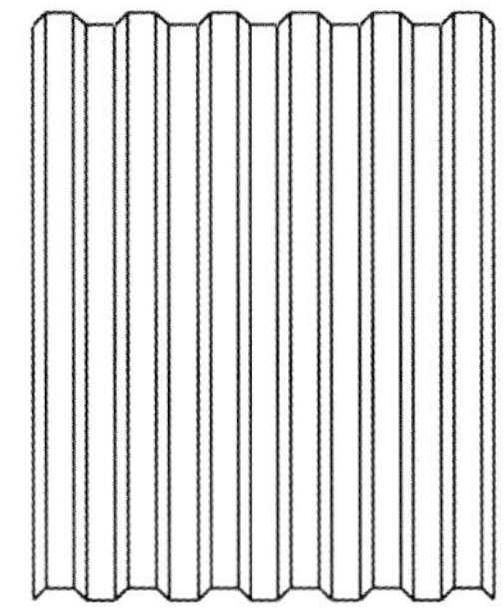

11. Hurricane - Metal Panel

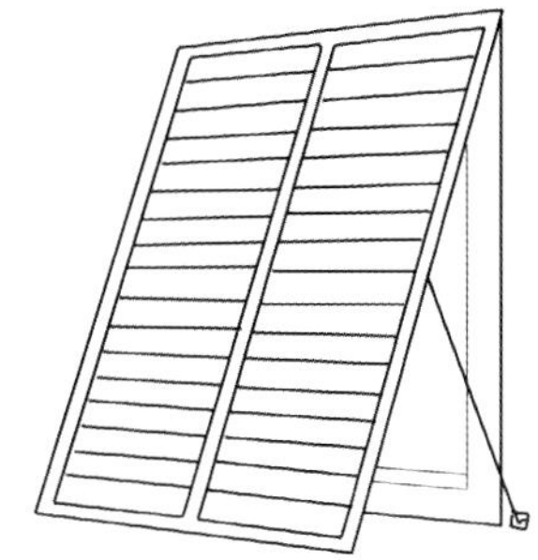

12. Hurricane - Bahama or Bermuda

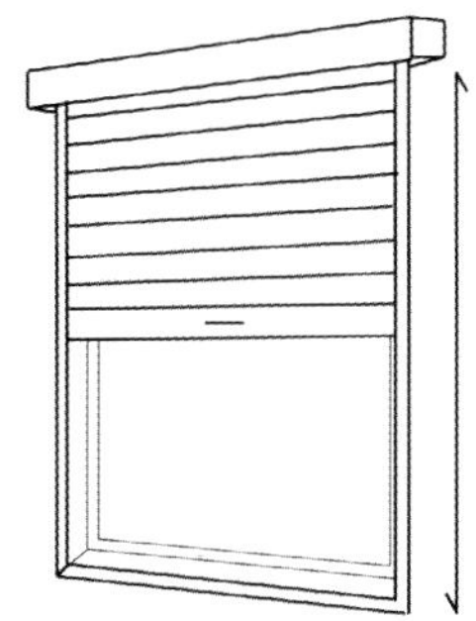

13. Hurricane - Roll-up

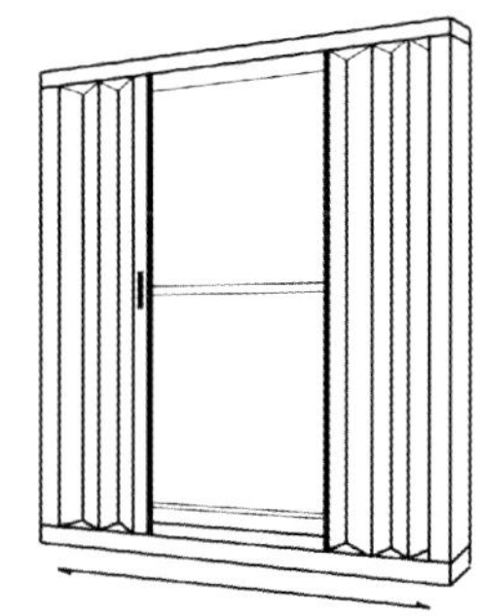

14. Hurricane - Accordion

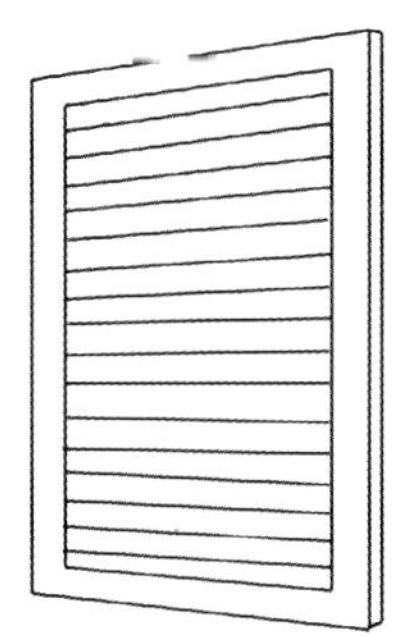

15. Hurricane - Adjustable Louver Inset

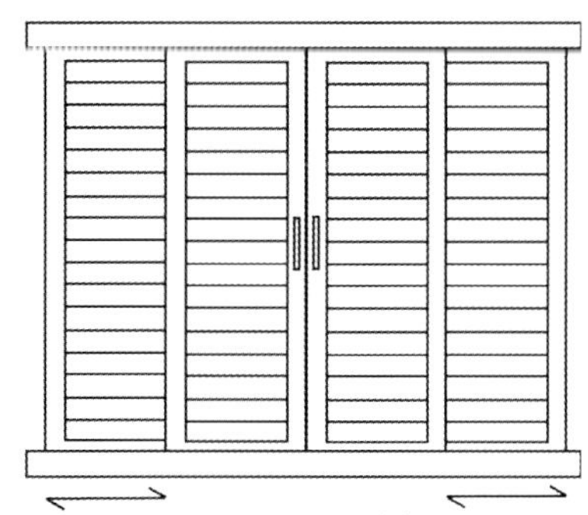

16. Hurricane - Sliding

Photographs of Exterior Shutters

The sections that follow are sorted by the design type. The photographs are of exterior shutters on structures located in various areas of the United States. You will see these shutters doing their jobs either as decorative or working models—or both. Many of them have weathered numerous years and diverse storms containing high winds and flying debris. The city and state where the pictures were taken are shown under each photograph simply for orientation. Within each section, the pictures appear in the order they were taken.

Section 1. Colonial Exterior Shutter, Creative Design

As I searched for exterior shutters, the majority of shutters were the typical exterior shutters as shown in Sections 2 through 16. Here in Section 1 are pictures of exterior shutters with individual and unique designs that have been independently crafted and/or personalized. It's apparent that most of these shutters are for decoration and are not meant to protect the windows they adorn.

Colonial Exterior Shutter, Creative Design
The louver shutter has been decorated with a curved cross bar. The shutters have hinges, so they are operable shutters.
Kansas City

Colonial Exterior Shutter, Creative Design
Look closely at this board shutter surface and you will see that it has been embossed.
Mackinac Island, Michigan

Colonial Exterior Shutter, Creative Design
The board shutter has a "club"-shaped opening cut out near the top.
Kansas City

Colonial Exterior Shutter, Creative Design
The board and batten shutter has a decorative cut down the center.
Kansas City

Colonial Exterior Shutter, Creative Design
The louver and panel shutters have a "spade"-shaped cutout near the top.
Kansas City

Colonial Exterior Shutter, Creative Design
The board and batten shutters have a "spade"-shaped cutout near the top.
Kansas City

Colonial Exterior Shutter, Creative Design
The shutters are a combination board and panel design with a "propeller"-shaped cutout near the top. They have dog/holdbacks mounted at the bottom.
Kansas City

Colonial Exterior Shutter detail, Creative Design
Kansas City

Colonial Exterior Shutter, Creative Design
The decorative shutters have an ornate cut at the top and across the center. The paint colors highlight this feature.
Lewisville, Texas

Colonial Exterior Shutter, Creative Design
The decorative board shutters have a heart cut near the top, and the edges of the shutters have been rounded.
Gatesville, Texas

Colonial Exterior Shutter, Creative Design
The slim decorative board shutters have a batten down the center, and three diagonal battens at the bottom.
Gatesville, Texas

Colonial Exterior Shutter, Creative Design
Decorative board shutters enlarge and lengthen the appearance of the window.
Crawford, Texas

Colonial Exterior Shutter, Creative Design
The decorative shutters have a light and airy appearance and dress up a plain window.
Gatesville, Texas

Colonial Exterior Shutter, Creative Design
One set of shutters extends between the windows on the first and the second floors.
Florida Keys

Colonial Exterior Shutter, Creative Design
Board shutters with hearts cut out near the top are on either side of the window. Inside the window are wide louver shutters that have a contrasting color.
Key West, Florida

Colonial Exterior Shutter, Creative Design
Shutter frames with mesh material installed in the frame has created screen doors.
Key West, Florida

Colonial Exterior Shutter, Creative Design
The windows have board shutters with diamond cutouts.
Savannah, Georgia

Colonial Exterior Shutter, Creative Design
The flat panel shutters have a "mushroom" shape cut near the top of the upper panel.
Charleston, South Carolina

Colonial Exterior Shutter, Creative Design
The flat panel shutters have a "tree" shape cut near the top.
Charleston, South Carolina

Colonial Exterior Shutter, Creative Design
The flat panel shutters have been painted to accentuate the appliqué palm trees.
Folly Beach, South Carolina

Colonial Exterior Shutter, Creative Design
The raised panel shutters have a "tree" shape cut near the top.
Charleston, South Carolina

Colonial Exterior Shutter, Creative Design
Board shutters made up of three boards of two different lengths are mounted on both sides of a larger window.
Folly Beach, South Carolina

Hurricane Exterior Shutter, Creative Design
Unique Bahama Shutters with two small windows in each shutter.
Folly Beach, South Carolina

Hurricane Exterior Shutter, Creative Design
Folly Beach, South Carolina

Hurricane Exterior Shutter, Creative Design
Folly Beach, South Carolina

Colonial Exterior Shutter, Creative Design
Squares cut out near the top decorate these operable board shutters.
Charleston, South Carolina

Colonial Exterior Shutter, Creative Design
Board shutters with designs cut out near the top trim the windows.
Charleston, South Carolina

Colonial Exterior Shutter, Creative Design
This handsome shutter was obviously designed exclusively to be used here.
Hendersonville, North Carolina

Colonial Exterior Shutter, Creative Design
The two boards that make up the shutters are cut so they form a diamond between them near the top.
Ashville, North Carolina

Colonial Exterior Shutter, Creative Design
Louvers at the bottom and panels at the top, with stars cut out near the top.
Lexington, Kentucky

Colonial Exterior Shutter, Creative Design
Metal shutters and bars protect this window.
Frankfort, Kentucky

Colonial Exterior Shutter, Creative Design
Two diamonds are cut into each of these black board shutters near the top and bottom.
Frankfort, Kentucky

Colonial Exterior Shutter, Creative Design
Louvers at the bottom and panels at the top, with crescent shapes cut out near the top.
Lexington, Kentucky

Colonial Exterior Shutter, Creative Design
Metal radius top shutters are used for doors.
Frankfort, Kentucky

Colonial Exterior Shutter, Creative Design
Two diamonds are cut into each of these green board shutters near the top and bottom.
Frankfort, Kentucky

Colonial Exterior Shutter, Creative Design
Operable flat panel shutters are decorated with crescent shapes cut out near the top.
Frankfort, Kentucky

Colonial Exterior Shutter, Creative Design
These shutters are lattice shapes.
Fort Branch, Indiana

Colonial Exterior Shutter, Creative Design
Board shutters with cutouts down the middle.
Princeton, Indiana

Colonial Exterior Shutter, Creative Design
Operable flat panel shutters have a lit candle in a holder cut out near the top.
Evansville, Indiana

Colonial Exterior Shutter, Creative Design
A flat panel shutter and a raised panel shutter with pine trees cut out near the top of each.
Princeton, Indiana

Colonial Exterior Shutter, Creative Design
Board shutters with two large hinges and an eagle on each shutter.
Terre Haute, Indiana

Colonial Exterior Shutter, Creative Design
Board shutters with battens near the middle and hearts cut out above and below the battens.
Bloomington, Illinois

Colonial Exterior Shutter, Creative Design
Shaped board shutters with two evenly spaced hearts cut out.
Bloomington, Illinois

Colonial Exterior Shutter, Creative Design
Gray flat panel shutters with crescents cut out near the top.
Bloomington, Illinois

Colonial Exterior Shutter, Creative Design
Green flat panel shutters with crescents cut out near the top.
Oak Park (Chicago), Illinois

Colonial Exterior Shutter, Creative Design
Board and batten shutters with design cut out at the top.
Orfordville, Wisconsin

Colonial Exterior Shutter, Creative Design
Board and batten shutter with a heart cut out near the top and one near the bottom.
Orfordville, Wisconsin

Colonial Exterior Shutter, Creative Design
Gray board shutter with designs cut out near the top and bottom. Notice the matching board framing the top of the window. The result of the added decoration frames and enlarges the appearance of the window.
Orfordville, Wisconsin

Colonial Exterior Shutter, Creative Design
Louver panel at the bottom, and flat panel with diamond cut out at the top.
Beloit, Wisconsin

Colonial Exterior Shutter, Creative Design
Board shutter made up with oblique boards.
Beloit, Wisconsin

Colonial Exterior Shutter, Creative Design
White board and brown batten shutters made up with wide battens.
Beloit, Wisconsin

Colonial Exterior Shutter, Creative Design
Board and batten shutters with a heart on each batten.
Beloit, Wisconsin

Colonial Exterior Shutter, Creative Design
Green board and batten shutters with large pine trees cut out.
Beloit, Wisconsin

Colonial Exterior Shutter, Creative Design
Brown raised panel shutter with white appliqué diamonds on the panels and white framing the panels.
South Beloit, Illinois

Colonial Exterior Shutter, Creative Design
Green board and batten shutter with a hinge on each batten, and a horse and wagon centered on the board.
Janesville, Wisconsin

Colonial Exterior Shutter, Creative Design
White board shutter with the horizontal and vertical battens painted brown.
Sharon, Wisconsin

Colonial Exterior Shutter, Creative Design
Janesville, Wisconsin

Colonial Exterior Shutter, Creative Design
Sharon, Wisconsin

Colonial Exterior Shutter, Creative Design
Flat panel shutter with small circle appliqué near the top of the shutter.
Shorewood (Milwaukee), Wisconsin

Colonial Exterior Shutter, Creative Design
Board shutter painted brown with white edge and a decorative appliqué.
Rockford, Illinois

Colonial Exterior Shutter, Creative Design
Shutter is made with two boards rounded at the ends and painted red.
Sharon, Wisconsin

Colonial Exterior Shutter, Creative Design
Rockford, Illinois

Colonial Exterior Shutter, Creative Design
Flat panel shutter with design cut out near the top.
Rockford, Illinois

Colonial Exterior Shutter, Creative Design
Operable raised panel shutter with design cut out in the top panel.
Rockford, Illinois

Colonial Exterior Shutter, Creative Design
Operable shutter with panel of louvers and a flat panel with a design cut out. Shutters at the right have radius tops.
Rockford, Illinois

Colonial Exterior Shutter, Creative Design
Operable shutter with a panel of louvers and a flat panel with a potted plant design cut out.
Rockford, Illinois

Colonial Exterior Shutter, Creative Design
Operable shutter with panel of louvers and a flat panel with a design cut out.
Rockford, Illinois

Colonial Exterior Shutter,
Creative Design
Thin board and batten
decorative shutter.
Wisconsin Dells, Wisconsin

Colonial Exterior Shutter,
Creative Design
Wisconsin Dells, Wisconsin

Colonial Exterior Shutter,
Creative Design
Board shutter with a "heart"
cut out at the center of the
shutter.
Wisconsin Dells, Wisconsin

Colonial Exterior Shutter,
Creative Design
Each window has thin board
and batten decorative shutters
and a matching flowerbox.
Wisconsin Dells, Wisconsin

Colonial Exterior Shutter, Creative Design
Board shutters with large contrasting colored hinges.
Wisconsin Dells, Wisconsin

Colonial Exterior Shutter, Creative Design
Flat panel shutters painted in contrasting colors.
Dallas, Oregon

Colonial Exterior Shutter, Creative Design
Four horizontal thin boards with equal space between and attached with three vertical battens make up these shutters.
Dallas, Oregon

Colonial Exterior Shutter, Creative Design
Red board and batten shutters with three decorative cutouts down the center. The back side of the shutter is lined with a board painted yellow so the cut outs contrast with the red shutter.
Wisconsin Dells, Wisconsin

Colonial Exterior Shutter, Creative Design
Board and batten with small round holes in the center.
Dallas, Oregon

Colonial Exterior Shutter, Creative Design
These "shutters" are actually boards framing the window and diagonal boards cross the outer area. They appear to be shutters on either side of the window.
Dallas, Oregon

Colonial Exterior Shutter, Creative Design
Four horizontal and three slender pieces of wood are combined to make a shutter.
Independence, Oregon

Colonial Exterior Shutter, Creative Design
Board and batten shutters that are radius at the top and bottom. The shutters each have two heart cutouts.
Independence, Oregon

Colonial Exterior Shutter, Creative Design
Three horizontal slender pieces of wood an equal distance apart are held together with vertical battens.
Independence, Oregon

Colonial Exterior Shutter, Creative Design
Board shutter with pine tree cutout.
Independence, Oregon

Colonial Exterior Shutter, Creative Design
Board and batten with oak leaf cut out.
Independence, Oregon

Colonial Exterior Shutter, Creative Design
Four slender pieces of wood an equal distance apart with decorative appliqué.
Independence, Oregon

Colonial Exterior Shutter, Creative Design
Three slender boards an equal distance apart with the center board shorter than the two outer boards.
Independence, Oregon

Section 2. Colonial Exterior Shutter, Single Frame with Fixed Louvers

Single frame fixed louver shutters have a frame containing a stack of louvers in a fixed position.

Colonial Exterior Shutter, Single Frame with Fixed Louvers
Mackinac Island, Michigan

Colonial Exterior Shutter, Single Frame with Fixed Louvers
Mackinac Island, Michigan

Colonial Exterior Shutter, Single Frame with Fixed Louvers
Florida Keys

Colonial Exterior Shutter, Single Frame with Fixed Louvers
Look closely at the installation of these four colonial shutters. They have been made into hurricane shutters with the addition of three metal braces and heavy duty hardware. This set of shutters wins the prize for most secured shutters.
Florida Keys

Colonial Exterior Shutter, Single Frame with Fixed Louvers
Florida Keys

Colonial Exterior Shutter, Single Frame with Fixed Louvers
Florida Keys

Colonial Exterior Shutter, Single Frame with Fixed Louvers
Two hinged shutters fold back and stack next to the window.
Florida Keys

Colonial Exterior Shutter, Single Frame with Fixed Louvers
The security for these shutters when they are closed looks makeshift but is effective.
Key West, Florida

Colonial Exterior Shutter, Single Frame with Fixed Louvers
The location and installation on the window frame and the use of mortise hinges raise the shutters away from the window frame. The matching color of the shutters and the window frame add to the pleasing appearance of this installation.
Key West, Florida

Colonial Exterior Shutter, Single Frame with Fixed Louvers
Florida Keys

Colonial Exterior Shutter, Single Frame with Fixed Louvers
Key West. Florida

Colonial Exterior Shutter, Single Frame with Fixed Louvers
The hardware and type of installation raise these operable red shutters away from the wall of the house when they are in the open position.
Key West, Florida

Colonial Exterior Shutter, Single Frame with Fixed Louvers
This window has a set of folding shutters that tuck into the recessed window opening.
Charleston, South Carolina

Colonial Exterior Shutter, Single Frame with Fixed Louvers
Shutters as far as you can see.
Key West, Florida

Colonial Exterior Shutter, Single Frame with Fixed Louvers
Winchester, Kentucky

Colonial Exterior Shutter, Single Frame with Fixed Louvers
Frankfort, Kentucky

Colonial Exterior Shutter, Single Frame with Fixed Louvers
The white casement windows and shutters are a clean looking and matching combination.
Orfordville, Wisconsin

Colonial Exterior Shutter, Single Frame with Fixed Louvers
A small window appears larger with the use of a decoration below the window and the lengthened shutters.
Princeton, Indiana

Colonial Exterior Shutter, Single Frame with Fixed Louvers
The style of windows, shutters, and a wall plaque coordinate this area.
Bloomington, Illinois

Colonial Exterior Shutter, Single Frame with Fixed Louvers
Lake Geneva, Wisconsin

Colonial Exterior Shutter, Single Frame with Fixed Louvers
Dallas, Oregon

Section 3. Colonial Exterior Shutter, Divided Frame with Fixed Louvers

The colonial shutters in this section have frames divided in two or more sections and each section contains a stack of fixed louvers.

Colonial Exterior Shutter, Divided Frame with Fixed Louvers
Mackinac Island, Michigan

Colonial Exterior Shutter, Divided Frame with Fixed Louvers
Mackinac Island, Michigan

Colonial Exterior Shutter, Divided Frame with Fixed Louvers
Mackinac Island, Michigan

Colonial Exterior Shutter, Divided Frame with Fixed Louvers
Mackinac Island, Michigan

Colonial Exterior Shutter, Divided Frame with Fixed Louvers
Mackinac Island, Michigan

Colonial Exterior Shutter, Divided Frame with Fixed Louvers
Mackinac Island, Michigan

Colonial Exterior Shutter, Divided Frame with Fixed Louvers
Mackinac Island, Michigan

Colonial Exterior Shutter, Divided Frame with Fixed Louvers
Mackinac Island, Michigan

Colonial Exterior Shutter, Divided
Frame with Fixed Louvers
Kansas City

Colonial Exterior Shutter, Divided Frame with Fixed Louvers
Kansas City

Colonial Exterior Shutter, Divided
Frame with Fixed Louvers
Kansas City

Colonial Exterior Shutter, Divided Frame with Fixed Louvers
Lewisville, Texas

Colonial Exterior Shutter, Divided Frame with Fixed Louvers
At first this appears to be a single set of shutters on either side of the row of four windows. At closer inspection you will see that there are two sets of divided frame shutters on either side.
Lewisville, Texas

Colonial Exterior Shutter, Divided Frame with Fixed Louvers
Crawford, Texas

Colonial Exterior Shutter, Divided Frame with Fixed Louvers
Crawford, Texas

Colonial Exterior Shutter, Divided Frame with Fixed Louvers
Brownsville, Texas

Colonial Exterior Shutter, Divided Frame with Fixed Louvers
Fallets Island, Texas

Colonial Exterior Shutter, Divided Frame with Fixed Louvers
Galveston Island, Texas

Colonial Exterior Shutter, Divided Frame with Fixed Louvers
Galveston, Texas

Colonial Exterior Shutter, Divided Frame with Fixed Louvers
Galveston, Texas

Colonial Exterior Shutter, Divided Frame with Fixed Louvers
Galveston, Texas

Colonial Exterior Shutter, Divided Frame with Fixed Louvers
Florida Keys

Colonial Exterior Shutter, Divided Frame with Fixed Louvers
Florida Keys

Colonial Exterior Shutter, Divided Frame with Fixed Louvers
Florida Keys

Colonial Exterior Shutter, Divided Frame with Fixed Louvers
Key West, Florida

Colonial Exterior Shutter, Divided Frame with Fixed Louvers
Key West, Florida

Colonial Exterior Shutter, Divided Frame with Fixed Louvers
Savannah, Georgia

Colonial Exterior Shutter, Divided Frame with Fixed Louvers
Savannah, Georgia

Colonial Exterior Shutter, Divided Frame with Fixed Louvers
Key West, Florida

Colonial Exterior Shutter, Divided Frame with Fixed Louvers
Savannah, Georgia

Colonial Exterior Shutter, Divided Frame with Fixed Louvers
Key West, Florida

Colonial Exterior Shutter, Divided Frame with Fixed Louvers
Savannah, Georgia

Colonial Exterior Shutter, Divided Frame with Fixed Louvers
Savannah, Georgia

Colonial Exterior Shutter, Divided Frame with Fixed Louvers
Savannah, Georgia

Colonial Exterior Shutter, Divided Frame with Fixed Louvers
Savannah, Georgia

Colonial Exterior Shutter, Divided Frame with Fixed Louvers
Savannah, Georgia

Colonial Exterior Shutter, Divided Frame with Fixed Louvers
Savannah, Georgia

Colonial Exterior Shutter, Divided Frame with Fixed Louvers
Savannah, Georgia

Colonial Exterior Shutter, Divided
Frame with Fixed Louvers
Savannah, Georgia

Colonial Exterior Shutter, Divided Frame with Fixed Louvers
Savannah, Georgia

Colonial Exterior Shutter, Divided Frame with Fixed Louvers
Hilton Head, South Carolina

Colonial Exterior Shutter, Divided Frame with Fixed Louvers
Beaufort, South Carolina

Colonial Exterior Shutter, Divided Frame with Fixed Louvers
Charleston, South Carolina

Colonial Exterior Shutter, Divided Frame with Fixed Louvers
Folly Beach, South Carolina

Colonial Exterior Shutter, Divided Frame with Fixed Louvers Folly Beach, South Carolina

Colonial Exterior Shutter, Divided Frame with Fixed Louvers Ashville, North Carolina

Colonial Exterior Shutter, Divided Frame with Fixed Louvers Chattanooga, Tennessee

Colonial Exterior Shutter, Divided Frame with Fixed Louvers Folly Beach, South Carolina

Colonial Exterior Shutter, Divided Frame with Fixed Louvers
Clinton, Tennessee

Colonial Exterior Shutter, Divided Frame with Fixed Louvers
Winchester, Kentucky

Colonial Exterior Shutter, Divided Frame with Fixed Louvers
Winchester, Kentucky

Colonial Exterior Shutter, Divided Frame with Fixed Louvers
Georgetown, Kentucky

Colonial Exterior Shutter, Divided Frame with Fixed Louvers
Winchester, Kentucky

Colonial Exterior Shutter, Divided Frame with Fixed Louvers
Georgetown, Kentucky

Colonial Exterior Shutter, Divided Frame with Fixed Louvers
Shorewood (Milwaukee), Wisconsin

Colonial Exterior Shutter, Divided Frame with Fixed Louvers
Bloomington, Illinois

Colonial Exterior Shutter, Divided Frame with Fixed Louvers
Wisconsin Dells, Wisconsin

Section 4. Colonial Exterior Shutter, Combination Fixed Louver and Raised or Flat Panel

The colonial shutters in this section have frames divided in two or more sections. At least one section contains a stack of fixed louvers and at least one section has a raised or flat panel.

Colonial Exterior Shutter, Combination Louver and Raised or Flat Panel
Mackinac Island, Michigan

Colonial Exterior Shutter, Combination Louver and Raised or Flat Panel
Kansas City

Colonial Exterior Shutter, Combination Louver and Raised or Flat Panel
Crawford, Texas

Colonial Exterior Shutter, Combination Louver and Raised or Flat Panel
Charleston, South Carolina

Colonial Exterior Shutter, Combination Louver and Raised or Flat Panel
Frankfort, Kentucky

Colonial Exterior Shutter, Combination Louver and Raised or Flat Panel
Ashville, North Carolina

Colonial Exterior Shutter, Combination Louver and Raised or Flat Panel
Bloomington, Illinois

Section 5. Colonial Exterior Shutter, Adjustable Louvers with Tilt Rod

When the louvers are adjustable, they have a tilt-rod that runs down the center of the louvers. The rod is attached to each louver at the edge. The rod is installed on the side of the shutter that faces toward the inside of the structure so it can be reached when the window or door is open. This rod is used to tilt the louvers up or down.

Colonial Exterior Shutter, Adjustable Louvers with Tilt Rod
Galveston Island, Texas

Colonial Exterior Shutter, Adjustable Louvers with Tilt Rod
The tilt rod can be seen clearly where it runs down the center of each set of louvers. Each set of louvers can be adjusted independently.
Galveston Island, Texas

Colonial Exterior Shutter, Adjustable Louvers with Tilt Rod
Galveston Island, Texas

Colonial Exterior Shutter, Adjustable Louvers with Tilt Rod
Galveston Island, Texas

Colonial Exterior Shutter, Adjustable Louvers with Tilt Rod
Galveston Island, Texas

Colonial Exterior Shutter, Adjustable Louvers with Tilt Rod
Key West, Florida

Colonial Exterior Shutter, Adjustable Louvers with Tilt Rod
Key West, Florida

Colonial Exterior Shutter, Adjustable Louvers with Tilt Rod
Even though the shutters are closed, because of the light behind the shutter, you can see that the louvers are in the open position.
Key West, Florida

Colonial Exterior Shutter, Adjustable Louvers with Tilt Rod
Key West, Florida

Colonial Exterior Shutter, Adjustable Louvers with Tilt Rod
The louvers at the top are open, and they are closed at the bottom.
Key West, Florida

Colonial Exterior Shutter, Adjustable Louvers with Tilt Rod
Key West, Florida

Colonial Exterior Shutter, Adjustable Louvers with Tilt Rod
Key West, Florida

Colonial Exterior Shutter, Adjustable Louvers with Tilt Rod
Key West, Florida

Colonial Exterior Shutter, Adjustable Louvers with Tilt Rod
Key West, Florida

Colonial Exterior Shutter, Adjustable Louvers with Tilt Rod
Key West, Florida

Colonial Exterior Shutter, Adjustable Louvers with Tilt Rod
Key West, Florida

Colonial Exterior Shutter, Adjustable Louvers with Tilt Rod
Key West, Florida

Colonial Exterior Shutter, Adjustable Louvers with Tilt Rod
Key West, Florida

Colonial Exterior Shutter, Adjustable Louvers with Tilt Rod
Key West, Florida

Colonial Exterior Shutter,
Adjustable Louvers with
Tilt Rod
Savannah, Georgia

Colonial Exterior Shutter,
Adjustable Louvers with
Tilt Rod
Savannah, Georgia

Colonial Exterior Shutter, Adjustable Louvers with Tilt Rod
Savannah, Georgia

Colonial Exterior Shutter, Adjustable Louvers with Tilt Rod
Savannah, Georgia

Colonial Exterior Shutter,
Adjustable Louvers with
Tilt Rod
Savannah, Georgia

Colonial Exterior Shutter, Adjustable
Louvers with Tilt Rod
Savannah, Georgia

Colonial Exterior Shutter,
Adjustable Louvers with
Tilt Rod
Savannah, Georgia

Colonial Exterior Shutter, Adjustable
Louvers with Tilt Rod
Savannah, Georgia

Colonial Exterior Shutter, Single Frame with Adjustable Louvers
Wisconsin Dells, Wisconsin

Colonial Exterior Shutter, Adjustable Louvers with Tilt Rod
Charleston, South Carolina

Colonial Exterior Shutter, Adjustable Louvers with Tilt Rod
Charleston, South Carolina

Colonial Exterior Shutter, Adjustable Louvers with Tilt Rod
Turkey Run State Park, Indiana

Section 6. Colonial Exterior Shutters with Radius Top

When shutters are installed on arched windows or doors they need radius tops. Shutters can be constructed with radius tops, or radius tops are available to be purchased separately and attached at the tops of shutters. These radius tops come in a variety of designs and styles.

Colonial Exterior Shutters with Radius Top
Kansas City

Colonial Exterior Shutters with Radius Top
Brownsville, Texas

Colonial Exterior Shutters with Radius Top
Brownsville, Texas

Colonial Exterior Shutters
with Radius Top
Brownsville, Texas

Colonial Exterior Shutters with Radius Top
Galveston Island, Texas

Colonial Exterior Shutters with Radius Top
Florida Keys

Colonial Exterior Shutters with Radius Top
Galveston Island, Texas

Colonial Exterior Shutters with Radius Top
When the shutters need to be closed, these shutters slide across the face of the windows on the tracks.
Florida Keys

Colonial Exterior Shutters with Radius Top
Florida Keys

Colonial Exterior Shutters with Radius Top
These shutters have a radius top that can be purchased separately. The top is then attached at the top of a colonial shutter. Radius tops come in a variety of designs and styles.
Florida Keys

Colonial Exterior Shutters with Radius Top
Key West, Florida

Colonial Exterior Shutters with Radius Top
Key West, Florida

Colonial Exterior Shutters with Radius Top
Key West, Florida

Colonial Exterior Shutters with Radius Top
Key West, Florida

Colonial Exterior Shutters with Radius Top
The radius top louver shutters on this historic home have working tilt rods.
Key West, Florida

Colonial Exterior Shutters with Radius Top
Key West, Florida

Colonial Exterior Shutters
with Radius Top
Clinton, Tennessee

Colonial Exterior Shutters
with Radius Top
Winchester, Kentucky

Colonial Exterior Shutters with Radius Top
Frankfort, Kentucky

Section 7. Colonial Exterior Shutter, Raised or Flat Panel

Shutter frames that contain one or more panels have no louvers. The frame contains panels that are raised or flat and are made in various configurations.

Colonial Exterior Shutter, Raised or Flat Panel
Kansas City

Colonial Exterior Shutter, Raised or Flat Panel
Mackinac Island, Michigan

Colonial Exterior Shutter, Raised or Flat Panel
Kansas City

Colonial Exterior Shutter, Raised or Flat Panel
Kansas City

Colonial Exterior Shutter, Raised or Flat Panel
Kansas City

Colonial Exterior Shutter, Raised or Flat Panel
Kansas City

Colonial Exterior Shutter, Raised or Flat Panel
Lewisville, Texas

Colonial Exterior Shutter, Raised or Flat Panel
Lewisville, Texas

Colonial Exterior Shutter, Raised or Flat Panel
Lewisville, Texas

Colonial Exterior Shutter, Raised or Flat Panel
Lewisville, Texas

Colonial Exterior Shutter, Raised or Flat Panel
Lewisville, Texas

Colonial Exterior Shutter, Raised or Flat Panel
Lewisville, Texas

Colonial Exterior Shutter, Raised or Flat Panel
Lewisville, Texas

Colonial Exterior Shutter,
Raised or Flat Panel
Crawford, Texas

Colonial Exterior Shutter, Raised or Flat Panel
Los Fresnos, Texas – Flat Panel

Colonial Exterior Shutter,
Raised or Flat Panel
Brownsville, Texas

Colonial Exterior Shutter, Raised or Flat Panel
Florida Keys

Colonial Exterior Shutter,
Raised or Flat Panel
If you look closely at the panels you will see that they are elegantly engraved.
Los Fresnos, Texas

Colonial Exterior Shutter, Raised or Flat Panel
Savannah, Georgia

Colonial Exterior Shutter,
Raised or Flat Panel
Savannah, Georgia

Colonial Exterior Shutter,
Raised or Flat Panel
Savannah, Georgia

Colonial Exterior Shutter,
Raised or Flat Panel
Savannah, Georgia

Colonial Exterior Shutter, Raised or Flat Panel
Beaufort, South Carolina

Colonial Exterior Shutter, Raised or Flat Panel
Savannah, Georgia

Colonial Exterior Shutter, Raised or Flat Panel
Beaufort, South Carolina

Colonial Exterior Shutter, Raised or Flat Panel
Savannah, Georgia

Colonial Exterior Shutter, Raised or Flat Panel
Charleston, South Carolina

Colonial Exterior Shutter,
Raised or Flat Panel
Charleston, South Carolina

Colonial Exterior Shutter,
Raised or Flat Panel
Charleston, South Carolina

Colonial Exterior Shutter, Raised or Flat Panel
Charleston, South Carolina

Colonial Exterior Shutter, Raised or Flat Panel
Charleston, South Carolina

Colonial Exterior Shutter, Raised or Flat Panel
Charleston, South Carolina

Colonial Exterior Shutter,
Raised or Flat Panel
Charleston, South Carolina

Colonial Exterior Shutter,
Raised or Flat Panel
Charleston, South Carolina

Colonial Exterior Shutter, Raised or Flat Panel
Charleston, South Carolina

Colonial Exterior Shutter, Raised or Flat Panel
Charleston, South Carolina

Colonial Exterior Shutter, Raised or Flat Panel
Charleston, South Carolina

Colonial Exterior Shutter, Raised or Flat Panel
Charleston, South Carolina

Colonial Exterior Shutter, Raised or Flat Panel
Danville, Illinois

Colonial Exterior Shutter, Raised or Flat Panel
Bloomington, Illinois

Colonial Exterior Shutter, Raised or Flat Panel
Rockford, Illinois

Colonial Exterior Shutter, Raised or Flat Panel
Rockford, Illinois

Section 8. Colonial Exterior Shutter, Board

Board shutters are made up of one or more flat boards with nothing added.

Colonial Exterior Shutter, Board
Crawford, Texas

Colonial Exterior Shutter, Board
Galveston, Texas

Colonial Exterior Shutter, Board
Galveston, Texas

Colonial Exterior Shutter, Board
The right shutter is in the open position, and the left is in the closed position. To change positions, the shutter has to be disconnected and moved over.
Florida Keys

Colonial Exterior
Shutter, Board
Key West, Florida

Colonial Exterior Shutter, Board
Key West, Florida

Colonial Exterior
Shutter, Board
Key West, Florida

Colonial Exterior Shutter, Board
Key West, Florida

Colonial Exterior Shutter,
Board
Key West, Florida

Colonial Exterior Shutter, Board
Key West, Florida

Colonial Exterior Shutter, Board
Key West, Florida

Colonial Exterior Shutter, Board
Key West, Florida

Colonial Exterior Shutter, Board
Key West, Florida

Colonial Exterior
Shutter, Board
Savannah, Georgia

Colonial Exterior Shutter, Board
Savannah, Georgia

Colonial Exterior
Shutter, Board
Savannah, Georgia

Colonial Exterior
Shutter, Board
Savannah, Georgia

Colonial Exterior Shutter, Board
Savannah, Georgia

Colonial Exterior
Shutter, Board
Savannah, Georgia

Colonial Exterior Shutter, Board
Savannah, Georgia

Colonial Exterior Shutter, Board
Orfordville, Wisconsin

Colonial Exterior Shutter, Board
Charleston, South Carolina

Colonial Exterior Shutter, Board
Charleston, South Carolina

Colonial Exterior Shutter, Board
Independence, Oregon

Colonial Exterior Shutter, Board
Independence, Oregon

Section 9. Colonial Exterior Shutter, Board and Batten

Board and batten shutters are made up of one or more vertical boards with two horizontal battens, one near the top and one near the bottom.

Colonial Exterior Shutter, Board and Batten
Mackinac Island, Michigan

Colonial Exterior Shutter, Board and Batten
Mackinac Island, Michigan

Colonial Exterior Shutter, Board and Batten
Kansas City

Colonial Exterior Shutter, Board and Batten
Mackinac Island, Michigan

Colonial Exterior Shutter, Board and Batten
Kansas City

Colonial Exterior Shutter,
Board and Batten
Kansas City

Colonial Exterior Shutter,
Board and Batten
Lewisville, Texas

Colonial Exterior Shutter,
Board and Batten
Lewisville, Texas

Colonial Exterior Shutter,
Board and Batten
Lewisville, Texas

Colonial Exterior Shutter,
Board and Batten
Lewisville, Texas

Colonial Exterior Shutter,
Board and Batten
Crawford, Texas

Colonial Exterior Shutter, Board and Batten
Crawford, Texas

Colonial Exterior Shutter, Board and Batten
Aransas Pass, Texas

Colonial Exterior Shutter, Board and Batten
Mission, Texas

Colonial Exterior Shutter, Board and Batten
Aransas Pass, Texas

Colonial Exterior Shutter, Board and Batten
Rockport, Texas

Colonial Exterior Shutter, Board and Batten
Florida Keys

Colonial Exterior Shutter, Board and Batten
Rockport, Texas

Colonial Exterior Shutter, Board and Batten
Florida Keys

Colonial Exterior Shutter, Board and Batten
Florida Keys

Colonial Exterior Shutter, Board and Batten
Key West, Florida

Colonial Exterior Shutter, Board and Batten
Savannah, Georgia

Colonial Exterior Shutter, Board and Batten
Savannah, Georgia

Colonial Exterior Shutter, Board and Batten
Savannah, Georgia

Colonial Exterior Shutter, Board and Batten
Hilton Head, South Carolina

Colonial Exterior Shutter, Board and Batten
Charleston, South Carolina

Colonial Exterior Shutter, Board and Batten
Folly Beach, South Carolina

Colonial Exterior Shutter, Board and Batten
Charleston, South Carolina

Colonial Exterior Shutter,
Board and Batten
Bloomington, Illinois

Colonial Exterior Shutter, Board and Batten
Sharon, Wisconsin

Colonial Exterior Shutter,
Board and Batten
Orfordville, Wisconsin

Colonial Exterior Shutter,
Board and Batten
Trempealeau, Wisconsin

Colonial Exterior Shutter,
Board and Batten
Beloit, Wisconsin

Section 10. Colonial Exterior Shutter, Board and Batten with Diagonal Batten

Board and batten shutters with diagonal batten are made up of one or more vertical boards with two horizontal battens, one near the top and one near the bottom. There is also a diagonal batten between the horizontal battens.

Colonial Exterior Shutter, Board and Batten with Diagonal Batten
Lewisville, Texas

Colonial Exterior Shutter, Board and Batten with Diagonal Batten
Los Fresnos, Texas

Colonial Exterior Shutter, Board and Batten with Diagonal Batten
Lewisville, Texas

Colonial Exterior Shutter, Board and Batten with Diagonal Batten
These shutters are double shutters hinged to each other. This solves the problem of the roof being in the way preventing the operable shutters from being installed on both sides of the window.
Florida Keys

Colonial Exterior Shutter, Board and Batten with Diagonal Batten
Key West, Florida

Colonial Exterior Shutter, Board and Batten with Diagonal Batten
Key West, Florida

Colonial Exterior Shutter, Board and Batten with Diagonal Batten
Beaufort, South Carolina

Colonial Exterior Shutter, Board and Batten with Diagonal Batten
Key West, Florida

Colonial Exterior Shutter, Board and Batten with Diagonal Batten
Charleston, South Carolina

Colonial Exterior Shutter,
Board and Batten with
Diagonal Batten
Folly Beach, South Carolina

Colonial Exterior Shutter, Board and Batten with Diagonal Batten
Charleston, South Carolina

Colonial Exterior Shutter, Board and Batten with Diagonal Batten
Charleston, South Carolina

Colonial Exterior Shutter,
Board and Batten with
Diagonal Batten
Ashville, North Carolina

Colonial Exterior Shutter, Board
and Batten with Diagonal Batten
Sharon, Wisconsin

Section 11. Hurricane Exterior Shutter, Manufactured Metal Panel

Per FEMA Technical Fact Sheet No. 26 referenced earlier in this book, these are "Temporary, manufactured metal panel shutters." FEMA recommends the "shutter is installed in a track permanently mounted above and below the window frame. The shutter is placed in the track and secured with wing nuts to studs mounted on the track. This type of shutter is effective and quickly installed, and the wing nut and stud system provides a secure anchoring method."

Hurricane Exterior Shutter, Manufactured Metal Panel Florida Keys

Hurricane Exterior Shutter, Manufactured Metal Panel Metal panel shutters have been used to protect an access area. Key West, Florida

Hurricane Exterior Shutter, Manufactured Metal Panel Florida Keys

Hurricane Exterior Shutter, Manufactured Metal Panel Florida Keys

Hurricane Exterior Shutter, Manufactured Metal Panel Florida Keys

Hurricane Exterior Shutter, Manufactured Metal Panel Florida Keys

Section 12. Hurricane Exterior Shutter, Bahama or Bermuda

This design is known by both names and may differ from each other by the way they are installed, the hardware used, and their operation. One really nice benefit received with this style of hurricane shutter is that when they are raised in the open position, they provide shade similar to that of an awning.

Hurricane Exterior Shutter, Bahama or Bermuda
Fallets Island, Texas

Hurricane Exterior Shutter,
Bahama or Bermuda
Galveston, Texas

Hurricane Exterior Shutter,
Bahama or Bermuda
Fallets Island, Texas

Hurricane Exterior Shutter, Awning Shutter
Florida Keys

Hurricane Exterior Shutter,
Bahama or Bermuda
Florida Keys

Hurricane Exterior Shutter, Bahama or Bermuda
Florida Keys

Hurricane Exterior Shutter,
Bahama or Bermuda
Florida Keys

Hurricane Exterior Shutter, Bahama or Bermuda
Florida Keys

Hurricane Exterior Shutter,
Bahama or Bermuda
Florida Keys

Hurricane Exterior Shutter, Bahama or Bermuda
Florida Keys

Hurricane Exterior Shutter, Bahama or Bermuda
Florida Keys

Hurricane Exterior Shutter, Bahama or Bermuda
Florida Keys

Hurricane Exterior Shutter, Bahama or Bermuda
Florida Keys

Hurricane Exterior Shutter, Bahama or Bermuda
Florida Keys

Hurricane Exterior Shutter,
Bahama or Bermuda
Florida Keys

Hurricane Exterior Shutter, Bahama or Bermuda
Florida Keys

Hurricane Exterior Shutter,
Bahama or Bermuda
Florida Keys

Hurricane Exterior
Shutter, Bahama or
Bermuda
Florida Keys

Hurricane Exterior Shutter, Bahama or Bermuda
Florida Keys

Hurricane Exterior Shutter,
Bahama or Bermuda
Florida Keys

-lurricane Exterior Shutter, Bahama or
3ermuda
-lorida Keys

Hurricane Exterior Shutter, Bahama or Bermuda
Key West, Florida

Hurricane Exterior Shutter, Bahama or Bermuda
Florida Keys

Hurricane Exterior Shutter, Bahama or
Bermuda
Florida Keys

Hurricane Exterior Shutter, Bahama or Bermuda
Florida Keys

Hurricane Exterior Shutter, Bahama or Bermuda
Key West, Florida

Hurricane Exterior Shutter, Bahama or Bermuda
Key West, Florida

Hurricane Exterior Shutter, Bahama or Bermuda
Key West, Florida

Hurricane Exterior Shutter,
Bahama or Bermuda
Key West, Florida

Hurricane Exterior
Shutter, Bahama or
Bermuda
Key West, Florida

Hurricane Exterior Shutter, Bahama or Bermuda
Charleston, South Carolina

Hurricane Exterior Shutter, Bahama or Bermuda
Key West, Florida

Hurricane Exterior Shutter, Bahama or Bermuda
Charleston, South Carolina

Hurricane Exterior Shutter, Bahama or Bermuda
Folly Beach, South Carolina

Hurricane Exterior Shutter, Bahama or Bermuda
Folly Beach, South Carolina

Hurricane Exterior Shutter, Bahama or Bermuda
Charleston, South Carolina

Hurricane Exterior Shutter, Bahama or Bermuda
Folly Beach, South Carolina

Hurricane Exterior Shutter, Bahama or Bermuda
Folly Beach, South Carolina

Hurricane Exterior Shutter,
Bahama or Bermuda
Hendersonville, North Carolina

Hurricane Exterior Shutter, Bahama or Bermuda
Flat Rock, North Carolina

Hurricane Exterior Shutter,
Bahama or Bermuda
Hendersonville, North
Carolina

Section 13. Hurricane Exterior Shutter, Roll-Up

This type of shutter rolls up to be stored under a valence and out of sight. In the following pictures, notice the variety of valences in the installations.

Hurricane Exterior Shutter, Roll-Up
South Padre Island, Texas

Hurricane Exterior Shutter, Roll-Up
South Padre Island, Texas

Hurricane Exterior Shutter, Roll-Up
Los Fresnos, Texas

Hurricane Exterior Shutter, Roll-Up
Fallets Island, Texas

Hurricane Exterior Shutter, Roll-Up
Los Fresnos, Texas

Hurricane Exterior Shutter, Roll-Up
Fallets Island, Texas

Hurricane Exterior Shutter, Roll-Up
Fallets Island, Texas

Hurricane Exterior Shutter, Roll-Up
Fallets Island, Texas

Hurricane Exterior Shutter, Roll-Up
Fallets Island, Texas

Hurricane Exterior Shutter, Roll-Up
Galveston Island, Texas

Hurricane Exterior Shutter, Roll-Up
Fallets Island, Texas

Hurricane Exterior Shutter, Roll-Up
Galveston Island, Texas

Hurricane Exterior Shutter, Roll-Up
Galveston Island, Texas

Hurricane Exterior Shutter, Roll-Up
Galveston Island, Texas

Hurricane Exterior Shutter, Roll-Up
Galveston Island, Texas

Section 14. Hurricane Exterior Shutter, Accordion

Accordion shutters could also be called folding shutters. They slide across the opening from the left or the right and stack at the edge of the window or door.

Hurricane Exterior Shutter, Accordion
Fallets Island, Texas

Hurricane Exterior Shutter, Accordion
Florida Keys

Hurricane Exterior Shutter, Accordion
Florida Keys

Hurricane Exterior Shutter, Accordion
Florida Keys

Hurricane Exterior Shutter,
Accordion
Florida Keys

Hurricane Exterior Shutter,
Accordion
Florida Keys

Hurricane Exterior Shutter,
Accordion
Florida Keys

Hurricane Exterior Shutter, Accordion
Florida Keys

Hurricane Exterior Shutter,
Accordion
Florida Keys

Hurricane Exterior Shutter, Accordion
Florida Keys

Hurricane Exterior Shutter, Accordion
Florida Keys

Hurricane Exterior Shutter, Accordion
Florida Keys

Hurricane Exterior Shutter, Accordion
Unlike most shutters, these accordion shutters are made of clear material. The shutters were installed just days before the picture was taken.
Florida Keys

Hurricane Exterior Shutter, Accordion
These accordion shutters are made of clear material.
Florida Keys

Hurricane Exterior Shutter, Accordion
Florida Keys

Hurricane Exterior Shutter, Accordion
Florida Keys

Section 15. Hurricane, Adjustable Louver Inset

Adjustable louver shutters are either installed over the entire opening or solely inside the casing. Usually the louvers can be tilted to be in the open or closed position.

Hurricane, Adjustable Louver Inset
Los Fresnos, Texas

Hurricane, Adjustable Louver Inset
Aransas Pass, Texas

Hurricane, Adjustable Louver Inset
Aransas Pass, Texas

Hurricane, Adjustable Louver Inset
Aransas Pass, Texas

Hurricane, Adjustable
Louver Inset
Fallets Island, Texas

Hurricane, Adjustable Louver Inset
Fallets Island, Texas

Hurricane, Adjustable Louver Inset
Galveston, Texas

Hurricane, Adjustable Louver Inset
Key West, Florida

Hurricane, Adjustable Louver Inset
In this view you can see how recessed these louvers are in the window casing.
Key West, Florida

Hurricane, Adjustable Louver Inset
Each opening on this church steeple has a set of louvers.
Key West, Florida

Hurricane, Adjustable Louver Inset
Key West, Florida

Hurricane, Adjustable Louver Inset
Florida Keys

Hurricane, Adjustable Louver Inset
Key West, Florida

Hurricane, Adjustable Louver Inset
Key West, Florida

Section 16. Hurricane Exterior Shutter, Sliding

The design of the shutters is colonial, but the type of installation creates hurricane shutters. The shutters are installed in a track at the top and bottom of the window. They slide into position to cover the window and away from the window when not in use. You will see a few variations to this type of installation.

Hurricane Exterior Shutter, Sliding
Galveston Island, Texas

Hurricane Exterior Shutter, Sliding
Florida Keys

Hurricane Exterior Shutter, Sliding
Florida Keys

Hurricane Exterior Shutter, Sliding
Galveston Island, Texas

Hurricane Exterior Shutter, Sliding
Florida Keys

Hurricane Exterior Shutter, Sliding
Florida Keys

Hurricane Exterior Shutter, Sliding
Florida Keys

Hurricane Exterior Shutter, Sliding
Florida Keys

Hurricane Exterior Shutter, Sliding
Florida Keys

Hurricane Exterior
Shutter, Sliding
Florida Keys

Hurricane Exterior Shutter, Sliding
Florida Keys

Hurricane
Exterior Shutter,
Sliding
Florida Keys

Hurricane Exterior Shutter, Sliding
Florida Keys

Hurricane Exterior
Shutter, Sliding
Florida Keys

Hurricane Exterior Shutter, Sliding
Florida Keys

Hurricane Exterior
Shutter, Sliding
Florida Keys

Hurricane Exterior Shutter, Sliding
Florida Keys

Hurricane Exterior Shutter, Sliding
Florida Keys

Hurricane Exterior Shutter,
Sliding
Florida Keys

Hurricane Exterior Shutter, Sliding
Florida Keys

Hurricane Exterior Shutter, Sliding
The shutters are stacked in front of each other inside the tracks when they are not covering the window.
Florida Keys

Dormers and Shutters

I found several situations where exterior shutters and dormers were together. Since this book is about exterior shutters and my previous book was about dormers I thought I would present pictures of them together and identify each. See if you can identify them before reading the caption with each picture. I found some dormers and shutters are identified by different names, so I used them all, such as "flat/shed/box" dormers or hurricane "Bahama/Bermuda" shutters.

Dormers and Shutters
Brownsville, Texas – Dormer: Gable with extended roof. Shutter: These appear to be permanently installed louver.

Dormers and Shutters
South Padre Island, Texas

Dormers and Shutters
Dormer: Gable. Shutter: Colonial unique design.
Aransas Pass, Texas

Dormers and Shutters
Dormer: Hipped. Shutter: Hurricane Bahama/Bermuda.
South Padre Island, Texas

Dormers and Shutters
Dormer: Pediment/triangle with steep pitch. Shutter: Inset adjustable louver.
Rockport, Texas

Dormers and Shutters
Dormer: Gable with slightly extended roof and enclosed eves. Shutter: Hurricane Roll-up.
Galveston Island, Texas

Dormers and Shutters
Dormer: Gable with extended roof. Shutter: Colonial, single and double panel louver.
Galveston, Texas

Dormers and Shutters
Dormer: Hipped. Shutter: Hurricane Bahama/Bermuda.
Galveston Island, Texas

Dormers and Shutters
Dormer: Gable with slightly extended roof. Shutter: Hurricane Bahama/Bermuda.
Florida Keys

Dormers and Shutters
Dormer: Through-the-cornice/wall. Shutter: Hurricane Bahama/Bermuda.
Florida Keys

Dormers and Shutters
Dormer: Gable with enclosed eves. Shutter: Hurricane Accordion.
Florida Keys

Dormers and Shutters
Dormer: Gable with slightly extended roof. Shutter: Colonial single panel louver with bars.
Florida Keys

Dormers and Shutters
Dormer: Hipped. Shutter: Hurricane Bahama/Bermuda.
Florida Keys

Dormers and Shutters
Dormer: Gable pediment/triangle. Shutter: Colonial louver with tilt rod.
Key West, Florida

Dormers and Shutters
Dormer: Flat/shed/box. Shutter: Colonial Board.
Key West, Florida

Dormers and Shutters
Dormer: Gable with extended roof. Shutters: Colonial louver and hurricane accordion.
Key West, Florida

Dormers and Shutters
Dormer: Pediment/triangle. Shutter: Hurricane adjustable louver inset.
Key West, Florida

Dormers and Shutters
Dormer: Flat/shed/box. Shutter: Hurricane adjustable louver inset.
Key West, Florida

Dormers and Shutters
Dormer: Through-the-cornice/wall. Shutter: Hurricane Bahama/Bermuda.
Key West, Florida

Awnings

Awnings are great sun-problem solutions. They are so versatile and are only limited by the amount of money you want to spend. They are used for decoration, distinction, privacy, shelter, signage, or just plain shade. You will find them on most any type of buildings—homes, apartments, condominiums, stores, hotels, motels, office buildings, and restaurants. They are found over windows, doors, porches, patios, decks, terraces, balconies, poolsides, driveways, and on RV's—the list goes on. Awnings are made with canvas, metal, wood, plastic, acrylic or polyester film. They can be fixed or retractable awnings. The retractable awning can be manual or motorized—some with remote control. For a great deal more information about them, simply search on the Internet for "awnings."

You will see a variety of awnings doing their assigned tasks in pictures throughout this section. The collection of photos is presented in the order the pictures were taken.

Awnings that are solid green with white trim are over the windows
Mackinac Island, Michigan

Awning over window
Crawford, Texas

Awning over window
Los Fresnos, Texas

Awning and shutters on window
Key West, Florida

Large striped awning over one window
Savannah, Georgia

Awning over main entrance doorway
Savannah, Georgia

Awnings over windows the length of the house
Savannah, Georgia

Awning over windows
Ashville, North Carolina

Awnings over windows
Rarity Ridge (near Oak Ridge), Tennessee

Awning over window
Rarity Ridge (near Oak Ridge), Tennessee

Awnings over windows and door
Ashville, North Carolina

Awning over office door
Corbin, Kentucky

Awning over window
Corbin, Kentucky

Awnings over restaurant windows
Corbin, Kentucky

One awning over store, eight windows and a door
Corbin, Kentucky

Awning with name of business
over door
Corbin, Kentucky

Awning with name of business
over door
Corbin, Kentucky

Awning over door
Corbin, Kentucky

Striped awning over a set of windows
Corbin, Kentucky

One awning over windows and door
Corbin, Kentucky

Awning over a window
Winchester, Kentucky

One awning over seven restaurant windows
Corbin, Kentucky

Awning
Winchester, Kentucky

Awning over a front door
Winchester, Kentucky

A street of store front awnings
Winchester, Kentucky

Awning detail
Winchester, Kentucky

Two awnings over two windows
Winchester, Kentucky

A large white awning surrounds a porch
Winchester, Kentucky

Awnings over dormer windows
Winchester, Kentucky

Awnings over windows
Winchester, Kentucky

Awning on a porch
Winchester, Kentucky

Awning on a porch and
over a window
Winchester, Kentucky

Awning on a porch
Winchester, Kentucky

Awning over a window on
a dormer
Winchester, Kentucky

Awning over a window on
a dormer
Winchester, Kentucky

Dome awning
Lexington, Kentucky

Awning over a door
Lexington, Kentucky

Awning over a window that
has louver shutters
Versailles, Kentucky

Striped awnings over two windows
Lexington, Kentucky

Awning over a window that
has louver shutters
Frankfort, Kentucky

Dome awning
Lexington, Kentucky

Awning on a porch
Frankfort, Kentucky

Awning over a window
Frankfort, Kentucky

Awning over a front door
Frankfort, Kentucky

Awning over the front of the house
Frankfort, Kentucky

Awning over a window that has louver shutters
Frankfort, Kentucky

Awning over a double window
Frankfort, Kentucky

Awning over a window
Frankfort, Kentucky

Awning over the front door
Frankfort, Kentucky

Awning over a window
Frankfort, Kentucky

Dome awning over a restaurant door
Frankfort, Kentucky

Awning over a window
Frankfort, Kentucky

Awning over an office entrance door
Georgetown, Kentucky

Four awnings over four windows and on the porch
Georgetown, Kentucky

Awning with a sign on it on the front of a store
Lexington, Kentucky

Entrance awning on a gallery door
Lexington, Kentucky

Awning over a window
Evansville, Indiana

Awning over a window
Evansville, Indiana

Striped awning over the front of the house helps create a front porch
Evansville, Indiana

Awning over a window
and front door
Evansville, Indiana

Awning over a window and front door
Evansville, Indiana

Awnings over door and window
Evansville, Indiana

Two awnings over two windows
Evansville, Indiana

Two striped awnings over two windows
Evansville, Indiana

Two awnings with scalloped edges over two windows
Evansville, Indiana

Custom striped awnings over the windows and front door
Evansville, Indiana

Two striped awnings over two windows
Evansville, Indiana

Lavish dome awning over entrance door
Evansville, Indiana

Awning over double window
Fort Branch, Indiana

Matching awnings over
the windows
Fort Branch, Indiana

Matching awnings over
the windows
Fort Branch, Indiana

Matching striped awnings over the windows
Fort Branch, Indiana

Awning over a window
Fort Branch, Indiana

Matching striped awnings over the windows
Fort Branch, Indiana

Monogrammed awning over a set of four windows
Fort Branch, Indiana

Awning over a window
Fort Branch, Indiana

Awning over the door to the porch
Fort Branch, Indiana

Awning over a window
Fort Branch, Indiana

Awning on the porch
Fort Branch, Indiana

Awning over a window
Princeton, Indiana

Two awnings over two windows
Princeton, Indiana

Awning over a window
Fort Branch, Indiana

Awning over a window
Princeton, Indiana

Two awnings over two windows
Princeton, Indiana

Awning over a window
Princeton, Indiana

Awning over the entrance helps create a porch with sitting area
Princeton, Indiana

Awnings on an enclosed porch
Princeton, Indiana

Striped red and white awnings match the tower roof
Terre Haute, Indiana

Awnings on all the windows
Princeton, Indiana

Awning over the window
Terre Haute, Indiana

Matching awnings over the windows
Terre Haute, Indiana

Matching awnings over the windows
Terre Haute, Indiana

Front and side views of the awnings
Bloomington, Illinois

Awning shades the porch
Turkey Run State Park, Indiana

Striped awnings over the front door and window
Bloomington, Illinois

Awnings over the windows
Bloomington, Illinois

Awning shade the front porch
Bloomington, Illinois

Continuous awnings shade the house
Bloomington, Illinois

Awning over the window
Bloomington, Illinois

Awning canopy over the driveway
Bloomington, Illinois

Retractable awning shown in the closed position
Oak Park, Illinois

Awning over a set of windows
Oak Park, Illinois

Awning over a set of windows
Orfordville, Wisconsin

Monogrammed awning over a front window
Orfordville, Wisconsin

Matching awnings on the front door and two windows
Orfordville, Wisconsin

Striped awning over a window
Orfordville, Wisconsin

Awning over a window
Orfordville, Wisconsin

Matching striped awnings over windows above and below
Beloit, Wisconsin

Matching windows with awnings and colonial shutters
Beloit, Wisconsin

View of awnings from the front and the side
Beloit, Wisconsin

Awning with flower basket
Beloit, Wisconsin

Awnings over windows
Beloit, Wisconsin

Awning over front picture window
Beloit, Wisconsin

Awning over front door and side view of awning on the window
Beloit, Wisconsin

Bahama hurricane shutters used as awnings
Beloit, Wisconsin

Awnings over side windows
Beloit, Wisconsin

Awning over the front door and stoop
Beloit, Wisconsin

Matching awnings over the front door and stoop and over the front window
South Beloit, Illinois

Awning over window
Janesville, Wisconsin

Awning over the front door
and stoop
Janesville, Wisconsin

Awning over the front door
and stoop
Janesville, Wisconsin

Awnings over windows
Janesville, Wisconsin

Matching awnings over front door and stoop and over the front window
Janesville, Wisconsin

Awning over front door
Janesville, Wisconsin

Awning over window
Janesville, Wisconsin

Awning over entrance door
Lake Geneva, Wisconsin

Matching awning shutters used as awnings on the windows
Lake Geneva, Wisconsin

Awning creates a sitting area on the front deck. Matching awning over the window above.
Shorewood (Milwaukee), Wisconsin

Awnings and louver shutters on the windows
Lake Geneva, Wisconsin

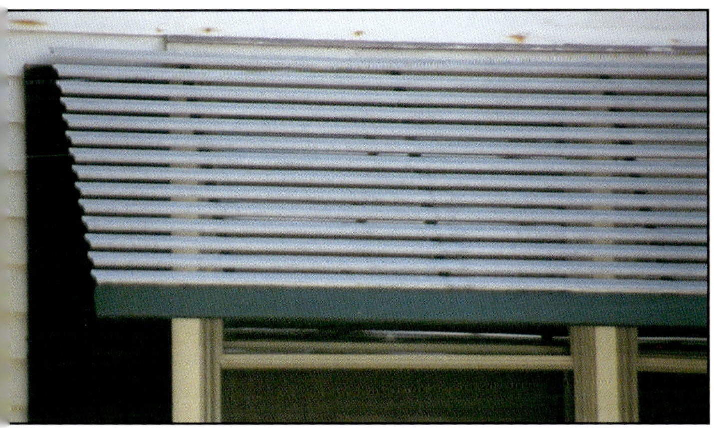

Close-up shows that when the shutter is in the open position it becomes a see-through awning.
Lake Geneva, Wisconsin

Awning over the window that also has a flower box
Shorewood (Milwaukee), Wisconsin

Striped awning creates a shaded sitting
area on the front entrance patio
Franklin (Milwaukee), Wisconsin

Matching awnings over the windows
Lake Geneva, Wisconsin

Awnings adorn all the windows
on this lakeside home.
Lake Geneva, Wisconsin

Brilliant red dome awnings over the windows
Williams Bay, Wisconsin

An awning and shutters add dressing to this window
Rockford, Illinois

Awnings add shade all around the circular roof
Williams Bay, Wisconsin

A striped awning peeks through the landscaping
Rockford, Illinois

Awnings provide shade under the through-the-cornice arched dormers
Rockford, Illinois

An awning over a window creates welcome shade from the sun
Rockford, Illinois

Awning and shutters dress up the window
Rockford, Illinois

Matching awnings shade the bay windows
Rockford, Illinois

Awning provides shade to the front picture window
Rockford, Illinois

Awning over window
Rockford, Illinois

Awning over front door and stoop
Wisconsin Dells, Wisconsin

Matching striped awnings on door and window
Wisconsin Dells, Wisconsin

Awning that works with casement windows
Wisconsin Dells, Wisconsin

One awning over front door and two windows, with a matching awning on the window above Wisconsin Dells, Wisconsin

Matching awnings over store windows and doors Trempealeau, Wisconsin

Dome-shaped awning over the front door and stoop Wisconsin Dells, Wisconsin

Awning over front door Wisconsin Dells, Wisconsin

Awning Trempealeau, Wisconsin

Striped awning over doors
Wallace, Idaho

Awning
Dallas, Oregon

Striped awning over set of windows
Dallas, Oregon

Awnings over windows
Dallas, Oregon

Awning over window
Dallas, Oregon

Awning over window
Monmouth, Oregon

Striped awning over door
Monmouth, Oregon

Awning over window
Dallas, Oregon

When in the open position the
awning becomes see-through.
Independence, Oregon